W9-AOW-406

# Slow Transparency

Wesleyan Poetry

# Slow

# Transparency

*Rachel Hadas*

 Wesleyan University Press
Middletown, Connecticut

Some of these poems first appeared, often in slightly different form or under different titles in these periodicals: *Agni Review* ("Fog," "Marriage Rhapsody"); *Ardis Anthology of New American Poetry* ("The Trial for Arson"); *Boston Review* ("Reconnaissance"); *Canto* ("Five Disguises," "Getting Rid of the Dog by Taking It Around the Mountain," "Making Sense of Salt Water"); *Central Park* ("Alien Corn"); *Chicago Review* ("Spring Green Still Creeping"); *Denver Quarterly* ("Island Noons," "Kaleidoscope," "Pastoral Assignment," "Praise for a Patch of Quiet," "Salt Citizen Re-enters City," "Triptych"); *Georgia Review* ("Moving Still"); *National Forum* ("The Colors of the Place," "On Poetry"); *New England Review* ("Island," "Journey Out"); *The New Republic* ("Getting Up to Look at Charcoal," "Women Are Best for Feeding Cattle"); *New York Arts Journal* ("Coup d'Etat," "Frieze Receding"); *New York Quarterly* ("Forgetting Greek"); *The New Yorker* ("Wish Granted"); *Pequod* ("Four Dreams about the Same Fortress"); *Ploughshares* ("Five September Hours"); *Poetry* ("Waiting"); *PN Review* ("Love's Geography," "Water," "Yoke"); *Prairie Schooner* ("Cleaning Fish in the Sea"); *Radcliffe Quarterly* ("Filial"); *The Spirit That Moves Us* ("The Last Possession"); *Three Penny Review* ("First Date in the Turkish Bath," "Speaking in Tongues"); *The Times Literary Supplement* ("Flying Home"); *Virginia Quarterly Review* ("Mountain"); *The Yale Review* ("Black Light").

All inquiries and permissions requests should be addressed to the Publisher, Wesleyan University Press, 110 Mt. Vernon Street, Middletown, Connecticut 06457

Distributed by Harper & Row Publishers, Keystone Industrial Park, Scranton, Pennsylvania 18512

Manufactured in the United States of America

First Edition
First Wesleyan Paperback Edition

LIBRARY OF CONGRESS CATALOGING IN PUBLICATION DATA
Hadas, Rachel.
  Slow Transparency.

  (Wesleyan poetry)
  I. Title. II. Series.
PS3558.A3116S6 1983  811'.54  83-14648
ISBN 0-8195-5089-2
ISBN 0-8195-6085-5 (pbk.)

# Acknowledgments

Among the many friends whose faces show through *Slow Transparency*, special thanks and affection are due to Stavros Kondilis, Barbara Waxenberg, and Elizabeth Chamberlayne Hadas—the best co-defendant, psycho-pomp, and mother (respectively) any poet could ever ask for—and to my husband, George Edwards, to whom this gathering of poems is dedicated.

Thanks also to the Ingram Merrill Foundation, The Macdowell Colony, and the Vermont Council on the Arts, all of which helped me with the precious gift of time.

For George

# Contents

## II *The Central Cameo*

## III *Locked in an Aorist Amber*

# I

## *The Idea of It, an Island*

# Journey Out

Say that you're lying comfortably under
the weather. Outside world? A passer-by
whose shadow barely skims the lukewarm puddle
of reverie you drown in as you lie.

Bruised but not feverish, you stretch and drowse,
minimally drugged against the pain.
An opalescent country's taking shape:
carpet, oasis, palms, a golden plain.

Pursed lips are blowing up a green balloon.
Spring; birthday party; training bra; the park.
Now gasp for air before the flashbulbs pop
their cameos and leave you in the dark.

Each dear desire is equidistant. Shut
your eyes and let a pin-pricked map direct
your journey. The arrival is what's hard.
Take off that aching carcass and climb out.

On nameless pebbles the ship grinds to a halt.
Gaggles of children are whisked out of sight
by mothers who replace them at the windows
(masked by lace curtains) in the looming night.

Only a single tavern is lit up.
With the swart owner and his pasty wife
you sit by a green wall and drink a toast
to this unheard-of life.

# Island

The idea of it
an island
in the center of a nameless circle of water.
Immediately you lose your bearings
no longer know east from west.
At the limit of vision a red sun rises
daily dyeing the mountains
that mark out morning and evening
dinosaur grey to rosy pink
but you still don't know where you are
and a terrible wind scours up from Africa
shoving along the shifting scratch of pebbles
sea that keeps humping itself to pounce and devour you
loudest black nights aroar with sucking foam
while on taut days of calm
nothing is spilled from the sheen of surface tension
but light
but light.

You can stay and squint it out
or twirl yourself into a compass
and attempt escape.
On one side will be continent
on another boundless ocean
scattered with silent islands
where no familiar chimney smokes
and peculiar gods are worshipped.
A caïque may take you somewhere
or a fisherman dipping in forbidden straits
may blow you up by mistake
with illegal dynamite.
But if you reach the shores of civilization
sooner than you suppose you will start to remember
and bore your incredulous listeners reminiscing
about the misty locus
of an impossible island
you left your life behind on.

# Mountain

~~~~~~~~~~~~~~~~~~~~~~~~~~~~~~~~~~~~~~~~~~

Coldly flushed at dawn,
swallowing sun each evening,
brooding visible world's end:
I finally take the challenge,
go to meet the mountain.

Windless sizzle of resiny pines.
Heat devils dance in gorges.
I fumble up and up,
Look down at a lineny wrinkled blue
cloth spread over an endless tabletop.
Over my shoulder
olive and carob trees
are such a quenching reassuring green
they seem to rinse the dust
from the glare of a survived
season now over, under.
I am above that line:
mountain crowning from water,
island touching sky.

At the shady waist of the mountain,
the Convent of the Annunciation.
And why climb any higher
than this huddle of whitewashed chapels,
its music of running water,
its arbor of grapes whose juice
is thickening to syrup?
Bees kiss fingers
sticky with watermelon juice and ouzo.
A mottled cat pads by,
buxom and noncommittal as the nuns
asleep or praying in their cells
whose silence may be saying

*Don't move abruptly, you'll disturb the bees.*
*Pull your skirt down, cover your knees.*
*Keep holy silence.*
*We go by the Old Calendar here.*

Harder to remember the descent—
too fast, on someone's donkey.
Before I know it I am at sea level
soaking in purple twilight, looking up
as at the moon now sidling from behind it
and saying to the mountain

*I know you.*
*I have been there.*

# Cleaning Fish in the Sea

Red and gold symmetry of Chinese carp
tucked neatly head to tail on a medallion,
blood clots, dribble of brain.
Fins red and blue as moistened water colors,
aquamarine with an electric stripe:
they waved like flags but now are flat in death.
Testicles. Egg lobes.
Throw the guts away.

The waves look small. They suck away and under
whatever stolen iridescences
I scrape off with my rusty knife and wipe
on the flat salt-bleached beach.
Iconoclast of visible holiness,
I strip the magic off before we eat.

For these divine mosaics turned to garbage,
I hope we pay in human coinage later.
And I keep thinking after their release
these scales will resume their interrupted
posts as single beacons,
chips in a pattern bright beyond all brightness
up in the sunlight; darkly visible
even in the chapels of the sea.

# Alien Corn

Turn to a blustery March where Cinderella
sits on a metal bedstead near a beach
sifting and sorting lentils. Ostrogoths
swagger the shingled village's one street.
Roaring of south wind. Vomited-up wine
splotches the floor near her corner.
Tiny red glass beads and shards of something
among the lentils slow her fingers further.
As in a fairy tale, the careful task—
to put together, to extract, complete
a testing chore by whom or why imposed
is unrecorded, as is the reward.
The needle may be pulled gleaming from the haystack,
the last lentil clatter clean into the pan—
she lacks the unimagined talisman
needed to pace and trace the labyrinth
bobbing perhaps in the slaty austere sea.

# Spring Green Still Creeping

If latitude and longitude should matter,
scene is a village yard. It features a sheep
butting, baaing, head caught in a basket.
Sparrows chitter on roof tiles.

A cat sneaks through wet grass.
The sea this year is closer,
the carved-out beach recedes.
Everything is the same and not the same.

I am invisible, I walk the beach.
I light a stinking rubber-burning fire,
nub-smooth sea-changed shoe-soles, clouded glass:
fuel gathered from the junkshop of the sea.

You couldn't sleep. It came to me to tell you
remember falling snow, the hills at home,
no colors, only motion,
all slowly falling, whirling, disappearing.

How could you sleep? The sun of March is wicked.
My arms erupt as baby fig leaves sprout,
scarlet and wet chartreuse respectively.
Conflagrations renew themselves.

Seven gulls circle over a burnt hill.
Fire has just zigzagged a piebald path up,
dividing black from green. On one side
toasted caterpillars, snails charred in their shells

are tidy hors d'oeuvres, so the gulls
fly over with faint gleeful cries
these terraces of salvation and damnation,
spring green still creeping round the other side.

# Coup d'Etat*

for Alan Ansen

## First Queen

The routine closes in upon itself.
No fresh flowers from the Friday market,
no visiting angels;
curfew hems me in.
Only the solace of muffled Berlioz
and Agatha Christie against distant gunfire.

## Second Queen

All my apple-cheeked downy-assed
lovely boys have gone to war.
No one can laugh with me at Noel Coward
or gasp at Wagner—it's dreary here alone
with no one to sample the hot and sour soup.
Those two too recent deaths and I'm bloody lonely,
soldiers, soldiers.

## Girl

From these hills' banality of green
and the flat vowels of democracy
I picture the flower-tossing crowd,
slogans swirling, sea-changes of state.
My knotted stomach registers
your exact place on this week's shifting map.

*Greek junta falls, 1974; Turkish invasion feared

Boy

Here on the island, tanks
lurk behind olive trees.
Every child has a grenade to toss.
Soldiers are ferried in from every province.
Let Turks beware! We shit on all the beaches.
Remoteness of tender flesh.
I am at a distance from my life.

# First Date in the Turkish Bath

In the hamam dim boomings, damp concrete,
sweat-misted walls. This is a different heat

from the dry brightness scorching visitors
over at the Acropolis. Bronze doors

clang shut: we have a private marble slab.
We lie down, clammy; I rub you, you rub

me, months of dirt shred out in grains.
Soaped, scrubbed, we sweat what secret dirt remains

out into blackish pellets shaped like rice.
First date. A last date here, would that be nice?

Neighboring bathers boom through the tiled wall.
A shriek would not be heard in here at all.

Languidly we stew in our own juice.
I picture Clytemnestra letting loose.

# Yoke

~~~~~~~~~~~~~~~~~~~~~~~~~~~~~~~~~~~~~~~~~~~~~~~~~~

*But when Necessity's yoke was put upon him . . .*
              —AESCHYLUS, Agamemnon

Tight as a package flying to the island,
how many times I've snuffed stale air,
craned and peered out the stamp-sized window,
seen tiny islands, infinitely thirsty,
soaking up the sea and never sinking.

Does a fish wonder what kind of cosmos
slants beyond its bubble?
Fish in a fishbowl, swimmer
out of sight of land,
I have become you both,
I have entered the zone of waiting,
have put Necessity's heavy harness on.
I bear the bulky apparatus
of not being able to choose.

Mainland behind, I heavily plough blue water.
The land recedes, the splashing picnic voices.
There is no way of knowing
how far the other shore is
or even if there is another shore.
I think of shooting upward,
leaving the water, the weight, the yoke,
and wonder already if I will miss them.

# Getting Up to Look at Charcoal

Night again. My hand molds
a living lump remote as Uganda,
unknown country across the mattress.
Ticking of hearts across unspannable distance.
Up at 1:30 to check the charcoal.
Scintillation of stars.
The smoldering mound, night-colored,
no visible interstices, still breathes.
Planets pass overhead, the dark garden
groans for harvest. When did this hurry begin?
Daily wind blows it at me,
opaque sky shines "Time, time!"
And in a meteor's streaking,
in the cloudy ooze of smoke into thirsty hours
I peer for auguries of dawn.

# The Lesson of the Elements

A few late stars punch the October night
with pinpoint asterisks. You lie awake
and watch the drama with your eyes shut tight.

Something is rising from the depths to make
flimsy flotillas of bubbles bend and burst.
Marshy odors linger on a lake

where various ancient treasures are immersed,
and swarming creatures from the water whine
around your head. The memories rehearsed

dully any day choose night to shine
glossily, foully, Xeroxes still wet.
First come the evenings mooning over wine.

Innocent, limpid, easy to forget?
Yes, but those hours trickled into years
of swamp you had to wallow through. Admit

what pool of wanting spawned the brood that sears
your tight lids now. The colors flicker higher.
The pictures waver and run down like tears.

But no repining. Now the stars conspire
to sharpen, deepen what's already known.
Even in dreams you get what you desire.

So that that summer, shining on and on,
granted one wish. Take fire or take air.
Of earth, a thirsty lump of vine-clad stone

whose source is deep in salt, learn to beware.
Loving and leaving it must go together.
Stay and the island holds you as a snare

rings round a captive animal. Beyond you is the water,
asylum to receive you if you fled,
whose cold blue mark would stain you ever after.

As fire wants air for burning, a deep need
to root yourself entrapped you in the earth.
These were the riders offering, each, his steed.
These were the four bright fruits on which to feed.

Count them again. First air.
Luminous past belief,
it gilds each stone, each leaf
until there is nowhere

except the sea to hide:
water opaque and cool
but inescapable,
circle the stony island floats inside

whose parched and patient ground
is firm beneath your feet.
Crumble it, it smells sweet.
Air, water, earth: you've found

the basics. Then the fire. First and last
the conflagration where all choices cracked.
So much for this rekindling of a past

you'd better put to sleep. To re-enact
the feeble sputterings can't ever end
the stubborn carboned nub, the final fact

time made, time mocks you with, and time will mend.

# The Trial for Arson

~~~~~~~~~~~~~~~~~~~~~~~~~~~~~~~~~~~~~~~~

*The Prosecutor, a Cretan*

With your permission, gentlemen,
let's reconstruct that night.

Moonless. Before her stretched the sea. Eastward
glimmered the lights of villages P . . . and S . . .

Westward the mountain blotted out the stars.
At such an hour all in O . . . were sleeping,

but she cautiously paused to listen at the door.
Only cicadas. Gasoline can in hand,

intrepid for a woman alone in the dark,
she stepped across the threshold, crossed the space

between the house and factory
and climbed the wall. This is how I surmise

the deed was done. Small flames would have been licking
the walls as the sky began to lighten. Back in bed,

she was up in her nightgown when the alarm was given.
Convincingly upset, but not enough.

Now, two years later, she is in the dock.
The proof of her guilt, gentlemen, to me:

How could this woman have been happy here
among you doltish Samians?

*With Fellow Defendant*

Sometimes the fellow prisoner almost becomes a confessor.
"Darling" (he takes you in his arms again),

"I'm sorry I've used up these years of your life."
"Oh love," you say, "oh yes, my love, I need you."

There was a time when you were more
to each other than fellow captives,

a time whose memory is all but gone
in this sucking slough of need.

How to remember? We scrounge and hoard our strength,
all energies scraped thin to last it out.

We last it out diminished.
The weight of this strange passage has flattened me.

Head hanging, I'm accused by those in power
of being who I am; of being here.

And they are right. I'm guilty: I am me.
Nor can appeals be lodged for time, life lost.

My innocence escaped them so they charged me.
My mitigating misery acquits me.

*Acquittal*

Pain of relief explodes, a sudden flashbulb
only inside my head. The world dissolves

to be put together later a new way
when all this has receded far enough.

*"Perastiká,"* they say—may it pass for you—
when only now has it passed. I'll never understand.

How our burden defines us
even after its lifting from our shoulders.

Nor do I understand why next day
we are back at the scene of the crime.

But the sense of occasion takes command as usual,
the villagers gather for . . . yes, congratulations.

An old man with dirt in the wrinkles of his neck
presses forward from a stable door.

Deaf as a post, he has somehow heard the news.
"The trial, my children? It's over?"

That will be what they remember about us.
And of our years here, full of light and air,

at this moment I think I will take with me
only this ending, but I will be wrong.

# Frieze Receding

Speakers in formula,
figures I moved among,
is it so painful
to put art on?

Simply slip an arm
back in an ancient gesture
as in a fold of the homespun
you persist in weaving.

Penelope for a season,
I unraveled the web, I know.
It is whole again already.
Don't grieve now

for one frivolity,
brief dalliance with disorder.
You are hereby out of time
again, forever,

safely sealed into
the blue and russet frieze
where I first saw you.
Flatten there, please.

# Waiting

Each afternoon now (the concierge foretold it)
sun visits us a little. The blue walls
don't know what to do with this intruder.
They toss a sunbeam off the lion's head.

On Monday the "time limit for refutation"
expires. No one had told us it existed.
When we're not in official anterooms,
papers stamped JUSTICE creased in our hands,

we sit around the emptying apartment,
refugees waiting for an exit visa.
Piled cartons; fruit we hope we'll never eat;
the two ceramic lions. Don't look up.

Our eyes would meet, we'd deeply breathe:
"Oof! The worst is over,"
and tempt our fate still further. Past the eye
of the storm these stirrings are deceptive.

What is peripheral to these weird weeks
keeps peeling off in preparation
for going, if we ever go. What's left?
Three books? You don't read. I don't read now.

What do we do? We see the evenings lengthen.
We follow earth's wobbly vernal passage.
The visiting social worker sunbeam
lights up our daily waiting.

# The Last Possession

Saint Francis threw his last possession down,
strolled toward the sunset humming a French song.

Years have undowered me.
There rests this treasure of silence:

a curve in the road, earth turning,
freesias glowing gold.

Acquiring control of the local means of production
we thought would tie us to land and seasons,

virtuous, feudal; but owning made a wound
festering with envy, opening deeper, deeper,

until the ulcered wherewithal dropped off.
Now these two lions, one gay, one growling,

terra cotta, inconveniently heavy,
are all that will leave here with us.

Domesticity then is this,
not sheets or chairs: two creatures

who take up room by one's shoes. Brother lion,
anchor me to the actual. Stay with me.

Now it's a desert I am talking in.
My own mate I have suddenly cast off.

## Getting Rid of the Dog by Taking It Around the Mountain

Swoop over rainless land.
Twin hawks circle the bay.
Driving around the mountain to give the dog away
light multiplied by sea daunts eyes like mine,
my gaze turns inland. Stony fields, ripe olives
parched on the trees, red rocks should give relief.
No, light alone, so clearly etched, inhuman,
maybe god's anger. Two tears, only water
in this bone island, wet my cheeks,
Patroklos watches in the mirror,
the dog huffs in the trunk,
going around the mountain to be given.

Peel life then to this core:
stone mountain huge a while and beautiful
those years it was the focus of our world,
landmark for ships or swimmers headed home.
Mere rock-hump now against the span of sky,
inscrutable in overwhelming light,
still it's the magnet for our final journey.

Poor hills we pass. I wish they could be watered
with the wringing out of what has happened here
so not one drop would be wasted.
May this trip prove fruitful
and the dog be happy
on the far side of the mountain.

# The Colors of the Place

The doctor takes me by the chin. "How brave
you must have been, my daughter, to come as into exile
and marry the remoteness of our island."
The walls are thin. Her husband's typing sheds
sharp punctuation on the pulled-out end of September.
"Your throat hurts?" she goes on. "Bad air from the sea."

Rather than meet her eyes I vaguely see
the flat port town from the bungalow window. Brave
new world gone dry and flyblown in September
that gleamed in June . . . Exile is true when exile
is palpable. You tug and feel a thread
toughly, invisibly stitching your life to the island.

Where is the olive green, unsullied island
I had imagined, silver toes dipped in a sea
of perfect crystal? The red
scab-dust of summer's end here powders brave
and cowardly alike. The town (packed tight with exiles?)
returns my gaze. Is this only the second September

I've spent here? Yes, yes: it was September
two years ago when they brought the doctor's husband to
    the island,
ferried him in at night across a wincing sea.
His sentence: "Write your blood-red poems here in exile.
You'll have a lifetime to learn what happens to the brave."
Of course their curse came true: his poems were ignored

by the islanders, including me. I read
Ritsos' Samian poems only this past September.
The years peeled off like onionskin, the doctor saying
      "brave,"
and me afraid to tell her I had simply found an island.
I had no Daedalus to waft me over the sea.
I stayed and lived it. Live it now. See now how like an
      exile

I crept to refuge. Now each piece of furniture means
      exile.
The too-fat palm trees bursting out of red
flowerpots on the terrace hide the sea
sloshing a block away. Mellow September
brings the last crop of tourists to the island.
They gaze and swim and mostly go. Those who remain
      think bravely

this coast at least is clear. Only the exiled poet sees
September rubber-stamping, taping everything in red.
Doctor, does bravery then mean simply seeing the island?

# Ut Pictura

The day came when I could
no longer paint injustice.
Light and water, mountainside and tree
buckled under misplaced weights of feeling.
Outlines curdled. Everything lost shape.
Language, then—bedrock, alpha, and omega,

strange new medium
that like a magnet snatches, fixes
shards from each day's journey.
Spaces, hardly signs
at all—boxed essences—
sidecar squares of primary
color whiz past for marking.
I flex my arm for intimate graffiti.

# Forgetting Greek

Translucent prophylactic, shield, interpreter—
language, I peel you off, stout rubber glove
I no longer need. My hand
is no longer callused by field work.
I recognize its uses.

I never knew I'd pulled you on so far.
There I was one day elbow deep in a tongue,
fingers furrowed with the unexpected.
Out of my depth, I started to pull back.
The soapy water of an alien way,
scummed pool, Narcissus puddle to gaze into
enchanted, distracted a young attention from
the bleak centrality of self. But now
here is my own right hand, still mine, uncovered,
square-ended nail-bitten fingers tapping the keys
of the language they thought I'd forget.

# The Clock of Afternoon

Long, slow, the arc of light eyed and re-eyed
to be absorbed, recorded, pondered on.
Friday morning we get up at dawn
to catch the bus around the mountainside.
Flat sky is building up to tragic rose
that slowly bleeds to day. The light: the same.
The distant village with the Turkish name,
so far that just an edge of convent shows
at the last hairpin turn, is still quite dark.
Cold breezes scrape the narrow cobbled street
blocked by the granite mountain from the sun
until an hour later. To return
puts that dim realm behind us. Next the work
of memory, to weave and re-create:

Cube of a room blue shutters cool to shade.
Lying down, we turn to one another.
Words stumble at the truth of *husband lover*
cherished past limits any names have made.
Siesta dream: an atlas. Riffling pages
of mountains and savannahs, brown and green,
bigger than any landscape I have ever seen,
I toil through space's lottery for ages
until the ghost casino vanishes.
Up, yawning . . . Ocean's zenith glaze has eased
a little. Stop the clock of afternoon.
There have been times I longed to snatch the sun.
Life, one long day, was made of littler days
to grab and palp and fondle as I pleased.

# Black Light

~~~~~~~~~~~~~~~~~~~~~~~~~~~~~~~~~~~~~~~~~~~~~

Having swum for seven
years in a foreign language,
I have decided to write
its dictionary down, out, word for word,
and illustrate the text with negatives.
One by one I hold them
up to the inner window.
Careful: these pictures speak,
these words have edges felt
through heavy velvet gauntlets.
A ray of dust
cuts cleanly in through the window.
Simple and pure as mud, the years drip off.

Sky: ink. Sea: milk.
That Christmas noon around the café table:
under a striped awning
white eye-slits, white lip-slashes
make faces.

I white out one or two
haloes and proceed
to turn a new leaf over.
But wait. First shut my eyes.

Translation of the pallor of that time
(I'd always missed the point):
the sky was black!
Crosshatched illuminations,
chiaroscuro gleaming neon,
details etched in drypoint—
to see in a new light,

bathe in the gaze's acids,
then pull dripping from the eye's deep well.
Eyes that peel the past's
fat off—or zip each layer of dialect
down to its body-stocking, simple babble . . .
I see a crusty palimpsest held up.
Chalk dust and pencil shavings are brushed off.
Then the purplish black
blubber diving suit
peels into stinging air.
Fresh as a Xerox, the wincing bones step forth.

That winedark sea has bleached to fine chablis.
Tingling, it yields transparent
secrets to my throat.

# Mouthings

Pale round pebbles, tongued and wetted, gleam
in the locked chamber, gather spurious heat—
icons of color ripe for kissing, plums
from the lawn of summer. Or easy
eloquence of bleakness in the autumn,
winter with its chill museum smell.

Who will volunteer to meet all eyes,
stand up, step forward, swing the padded stick,
and touch the great bronze gong?
Dark reverberations fill the hall.
The gathered listeners whisper, looking on
raptly, *It was time that that was done.*

Everything they hear is graspable
as words, can all be chipped or melted down
to currencies of tongue. I used to think
I minted the stuff myself—
polished nuggets ranged
cunningly in the showcase of my skull.

Hollowness proves me wrong.
Emptiness mirrors emptiness, a glittering
shell. Eyes and teeth
reflect reflexive surfaces' reflections.
Try it yourself. Put out a hand and take
a piece of fruit out of this bowl of light.

# Flying Home

Down milk-bright colonnades
the leper's bell recedes.

Shades lowered against the gleaming waste of ice,
I sit back, bathe in lukewarm acquiescence.

Dutiful, prompt,
strapped, doped, a little drunk,

squinting at international afternoon
I'll soon pass GO again.

And if these colored pencils, nose-drops, passport
should plummet with the rest of the huge oval,

giant time capsule soft for the shark's maw,
will a notebook ambered back to front with words

rescue me from oblivion?
Syrup of skittish travelers, fame. I yawn.

# Wish Granted

You said, "I will go to another land, I will
go to another sea."
　　　　　　　　　　　—CAVAFY

Far city, agora and games and temple
seen clear and whole only from this distance,
what figure threads your gleaming maze
foreshortened in strong sunlight?

In the guise of an office worker
I took a bus back to the coast each evening.
Darkness rose from the Royal Gardens
lit in flares by peanut vendors' fires;
couples spooned in the gloom;
gardeners resembled monkeys under palm trees.

Now the mask falls.
Cloud shadows mark these hills.
Green, green;
back in the treeland I want sea again.

In any landscape you will be the same,
life-size, a woman using this place up.
You say you're tired of azure skies?
So be it.

　　Roll of thunder!
Subaqueous light. Racing over a hayfield
you skid on wet grass, kick the bales downhill.
It may not all get in before the sky cracks.
Over a dead elm, lightning!
Wide sweet cool smell after weeks of drought.

It is not the rain, it is the idea of home.
Let it end here if it has to,
the pattern be lopped off with one hot jolt,
scorching silence,
and the wide hayfield tilting.

# Island Noons

I

All day there's nothing to do but sprawl in the sun
reading of fountains, meadows, hills, and groves.
Nothing to do but float in a blue
fluid through which forgotten
words shoot up like bubbles.

*And there that day when the great light of heaven*
*Burned at his lowest in the rolling year,*
*On the waste sand by the waste sea they closed*

my eyes as I lie on the beach
to block the glare. I will a cloud to come,
mask the fierce zenith.
It does come. It subtracts
shadows from the water.
Distant baby islands
invisible before
surface clear through the caldron of haze
simmering in the south.
A point of lilac light
thrusts from behind the mountain.
A hint of wind: the ocean will be colder.

I tell myself I knew this change would come.
Even in paradise
there must be shades of weather.
But the cloud passes.
A shadow on the sand
makes me lift my head.
Dizzily I squint
at Ariadne. Knock-kneed, light behind her,
shyly she smiles hello, tries on a flipper.
Her eyes are blue. I have no words to give her.

I put the poet down and plunge away,
the secret greenwood seared and quenched
and hissing in salt water.
Habit makes me scan
the skyline as I float
for any uprights
except the masts of fishing boats.
Gently they rock at anchor.
At the shell-fanged stones of the prewar harbor
I cling, drip, count the houses
along Poseidon Street,
their shuttered windows blank as new green blackboards.
The number never comes out quite the same.

Even years later
it's not much easier
to tell the truth about the place,
not to speak of its prettiness
as of a painted screen.
But let me try to put the noons
together and stand back
now the long day is over.


II

Cowled in routine, buying my bread at the oven,
perhaps I think the place will never learn to read me.
Each day I wear demotic
and when I take the mask off what is there?
Numberless gem-bright stones
dull on the beach as I bend to touch them.
Ironies and omissions stop my mouth like sand.

Caressingly they said,
"Look how devoted! See, she follows him
everywhere, as far

as the ends of the earth, think of it—
even as far as here."
And I'd reply, "But it is beautiful,
I like it here." (In Greek, *it likes me here.*)

Village, I learned your words but not your music.
I had no melody worth the taking.
I wore an ineffectual disguise—
blue smock, plastic sandals—
but must have seemed enough a local woman
after a while for them to ask, "You haven't
forgotten your first language yet? You will!"

No books but what I'd brought or once had read—
like Tennyson still floating in my head.
No mirrors but the water and the sky.
No verticals except the granite mountain
to punctuate the landscape. Shuttered houses
huddled together—still in fear of pirates?
Two rooms. The secret fetters. The loud ocean.

As if to tear a pastel sketch in two,
pierce it through,
this shine and ruffle of the sun on water,
and touch the bedrock of ineffable
truth that is waiting in an ill-lit corner
or would be if—no, here there is no dimness.
Quench the sun, still this world is washed in light.

I squint to try to see.
Years squint back at me.
Eden, oasis, exile, island, desert—
if I don't choose a name
what will become of time?
Untrammeled days roll down the moving oar,
plop back into the sea.

# II

## *The Central Cameo*

# Pastoral Assignment

Pastoral assignment: axes of the world
to grind to razor sharpness. Marry warp
and woof of body/landscape. Trace the map,
observe the cycle; better, make it up.

Go to the green world and come back again.
First set down childhood. Next comes poetry,
travel, romance—all shires of Fairy Land.
Oh, hold the real world off with either hand.

Futile migration, you say? Nothing learned?
Dust you began as and to dust returned?
Ah, but the house was magical. I taste
the outer rind and chew the tangy place,

grinding it ever thinner. . . . Savors rise.
A stream flows past, steam wreathing as it goes,
gilded at dawn by heavenly alchemy
(phrase I first learned here). And the hills reply

each day reflecting light come round again
to the same point and also not the same.
These deepening lines. Sun warming up my back . . .
No. Though lapped in light

and miracled today with winter cold,
somehow this place is not another world.
Cowled in its limitations, old and small,
it's cut to fit the cloth of pastoral.

# Love's Geography

The little fascist state that lives inside me
boards windows, doors, abandons buildings. Whole
neighborhoods are blacked out. The faintest fall
of light or sound could start a revolution.
Oblivion's one solution:
cut off from sense, to muffle and forget.
What masked guerrilla lies tonight beside me,
enters that zone
I thought was cordoned off from everyone?
Three o'clock. Four. The space seems empty, yet
stirs like uneasy water.

And presently the coverings unpeel,
flash tiny panoramas one by one.
Two married bodies, parallel, alone,
lie near the sea asleep, with salty eyes.
Crickets italicize
the silence of a leafy summer night.
Rattle of elevators. Siren's squeal.
The woman wakes;
quietly, so as not to rouse him, takes
her hidden notebook out and reads till light
bleaches the page. No answer.

Seven o'clock. Day rising in the mirror
reveals a bedroom and a shut-eyed face,
parts of a puzzle lost in alien space.
Seen through the window, dark against hot blue,
three pigeons nudge, bump, woo.
They look like elders on the wall of Troy,
frail but censorious. Perhaps they wonder
why we are here.
From that high perch, how small we must appear.
The aged audience awaits its play.
A pillow muffles it.

The cool and neutral seascape of the new
sets like a jelly with advancing day.
The lofty rooms, the muted cream and grey
        of wall and ceiling suddenly feel dark.
                For warmth I seek the park.
        Here baby leaves as yellow green as fever
are churned to mash by joggers as they go.
                Rancid river
that irrigates my inner map forever,
        some creature in your sour incubator
                is dreaming all this now.


        Succulent, pinkish, the infected air
dangles its secrets in a brown suspension.
Chance sounds and sights are charged with sudden
    tension.
            I drift toward home as afternoon wears on.
                Shovel scraping stone;
        rhythm of car honks; bottle caps that glitter:
fragments of language not for me to share.
                Perhaps cold rain
could rinse the neighborhood, make meanings plain.
        Heat ripples up from garbage in the gutter
                next to the house. I enter.


        Inside, a tactful twilight gives each piece
its boundaries of shadow: *you belong
here, chair: you, sofa, here.* Moving among
        these freshly anchored things, I acquiesce
                to gravity no less.
        For years, it seems, I've struggled to climb higher.
This new plateau should be a place of peace.
                Yet it cries out
my silent sense of what the fear's about.
        *Who told you you could have your heart's desire?*
                coldly inquires the house.

Speeding through spaces all inside a head,
I may fall backward into the old terror.
But dusk is changing colors in the mirror
    from warm to cool: now gold, now grey, now white.
        Such tender veils of light
        drape the day's waning and my tired eyes,
I'm gently wafted all the way to bed
        Years rise and fall
like waves . . . and now the unpredictable
    recurrent fountain of the soul's surprise
        bathes me in candor.


    I find that I have climbed a crystal stair
but from its top see nothing. What's the hour?
I note a glow of night or dawn; a roar
    of waterfall—or is it cars outside?
        Rinsed clean, open wide,
        awake but blind, I grope to find a clue.
The secret might be hidden anywhere,
        even in me.
How to decipher all the signs I see?
    Now I am listening as well. A slow
        melody on the piano


    drifts in and tells me who and where I am.
It's night. It's June. I've surfaced in this place.
I've crossed wide waters; rest in one dear face.
    If this pale palace sometimes seemed like Troy,
        old griefs can tell me why.
    Maybe today I poured their last libation.
I wake up in a world that's not the same.
        Ancient but new,
it's like the city I have found with you,
    both Troy and island in unfathomed ocean.
        I sit up and say your name.

# Triptych

Flanked by the yes and no
mirroring opposites,
encounter and refusal,
the central cameo:

my own unfolding body—
bloodless, aglow like wine.
The bird/heart now weighs in.
Head under coded wing,

all downy damp potential
to fly away? to sing?
to be? to beat? Remain
aorist, dear icon,

precious as captured time
and real as wind and rain.

# Making Sense of Salt Water

Try to see landscape whole and one wrong tree
marks out a hemisphere and spoils the view.
But near the ocean things obligingly
dilute into a noncommittal blue
matrix against which figures stand out sharply,
including me and you.

Like every island, this one's rich with runes
to spell a story out in weed, in water.
In turn we recapitulate the moon's
rhythmical tide-tug. We lie down, two stones
bared on the beach, or gull-like mew and veer,
flap heavily through sea-fog's long cocoons.

The tide flows
outward, washes back,
leaves clues behind
in a salt alphabet. No final answer.
These hazy days each time the sun goes under,
houses and boats are drained again of color,
smeared by the old confusion: sky with sea,
one coastline, island, ocean with another.
A new confusion pours you into me.

It hurts the eyes, I know, that milky glare
rising from nowhere. Still, stay near a shore.
In time we shall discover
another island, many islands, crowning from black water,
rolled between the maker's thumb and finger
out of chewy air.

# Five Disguises

~~~~~~~~~~~~~~~~~~~~~~~~~~~~~~~~~~~~~~~~~~~~~~~~~~

Deliberate footsteps braid
    a strand from room to room.
        Crossing the gloom
    she balances a vessel on her head
whose hidden contents nobody may know.
        Whatever deadly water
            bubbles and winks and threatens to slop over,
    no spill, no stain may mar
the glassy dark perfection of the floor.

I see you bear it too,
    cargo so breakable
        you must stand quite still.
    It may expand and fill you to your toes
or shrink until it's tiny—but it stays,
    gauging heat and fever.
        It mounts like mercury to measure anger
    and sometimes grows so tall
within you that you stagger, almost fall.

Curving along the sand,
    look! they have built a thick
        high wall of brick
    to separate the ocean from the land.
But if a tidal wave should rear its tower
    from that flat satin sea,
        the sturdy wall would crumble in a high
    advancing mound of water,
all elements smashed violently together.

Chronic, obscure, a pain
        in pockets of your life
                demands a knife
        at last. You lance the wound to make it drain,
sacrifice smoothness, scar the perfect skin,
        and feel it turning mild,
                the hurt you've nurtured since you were a child.
        Naked and strange,
to shuffle the old ailment off; to change.

The closet's full of clutter.
        What have I come to find?
                Ah yes. Behind
        a pile of ancient costumes I discover
the mask I used to wear over what was
        not quite a finished face.
                It pressed the features firmly into place.
        Habit by now alone
strong as a mask can mold the tender bone.

# Salt Citizen Re-enters City

Until tonight the salt solution thickened, thickened.
Wryness flavored everything I said.

An extra pane frosted, crusted over
pursed lips, layers of a life.

Now I return to the city rinsed of brine.
Dimpled or scraped surfaces shrilly glisten.

Black tooth-marks, burnt buildings
loom throught a bath of pungent mist.

The element I'm plunged in isn't air
yet penetrates each pore, so many arrows.

Haloed with stops and goes in red and green,
a smothered mauveish sky

not the right color for night or day
poses a question I simply must interpret.

## On Poetry

The sort of thing I want to prove is that
a twittering of pigeons out of sight
is enough to adorn a sunset. That the sea
unscratched by swimmers is as cold and blue
as thirstiest thought could daub it.

"Except for us, Vesuvius might consume
In solid fire the utmost earth and know
No pain." To which the utmost ocean
probably shrugs in generous indifference
its restlessly redisappearing ripples.

The green lawns, the old house
had best remain unprinted by our thumbs,
forever out of reach.
Cut life away from landscape:
still there's the poet scribbling alone

at a corner table smeary with graffiti.
(Over that table our eyes had often met,
saluted, and plunged back
to resiny depths of fire
that sent out signals through our watchful silence.)

Despite such flashes
the poet will be lonely. May imagine
a marble gallery full of characters
walking amd murmuring; a conservatory
spiky with potted palms to dump one's drink in,

chiaroscuro of moonlit blossoms,
hothouse smells, and laughter.
Otherwise, empty the hotel of people.
Board up the niches. Let
nothing but scratchy wind disturb the silence.

Forbid the old nostalgia
for what is recognizable,
intimacies of summerhouse and garden,
the contents of the labyrinth.
Tabula rasa or

embarrassment of riches—
either way it's a solitary business,
not what the wayfarer pictured
when settling herself behind that corner table
she first unfolded the map,

lifted her eyes to an uncreased world.

# Kaleidoscope

You ask the source of these transparencies.
Although each speaker is another self,
all finally return and merge to one
composite whole from which each fragment's spun.
Names, gestures, seasons, every kind of weather
one's friends can lend while losing nothing—these
are all I've taken. What is there to fear?
Busily I stitch a gospel, match
the patchwork of a city day, or peer
through blue arcades a single twist of year
has turned past recognition. Help me out,
chorus of voices. You know who you are.
Change partners: still it comes down to the same
symmetry dancing on its head of pain.
Label those angels if you can. As, whose
eyes brimmed with loneliness; whose anger found
its edge in shifting razor glints of color:
yours? yours? I put the instrument down. Meet
an eye, a pair, another, then another.
What lifts itself to meet me's pure anxiety
that in a twinkle flickers recognition.
It nods: I see you through the far end of the eyescope,
the you-turn, eyesore, telelooker, thing
to measure with, to gesture with, to distance
and finally to dance to. Parts are bowing
in little v's of colored glass. They itch
to curtsey, twirl, and strut their stuff. They die
to form a pattern—even words. Begin.

# Water

*If seven maids with seven mops . . .*

Water the level of the soul and water
the voice it finds. All voyages begin
when maids of time armed with their hefty mops
have swept the whole beach clean.

What led up to such a laundering?
Beauty. Terror.
What came after
rinsed the grit from the swirl of surf we stood in.

The fine-ground sand reminded us
of myriad bathings drained
but for a residue under
our arching toes. Slowly the cold slid backward.

Beach; voyage. On a lazy summer sea
I float companioned by a silent mentor.
We carve a channel between velvet green
hills to an unknown shore. I ask for time

and solitude on deck; they're granted me
as long as I acknowledge nothing's free.
Meanwhile an end-of-tunnel spot of pallor
illuminates two cameo figures seen

as through the wrong end of a telescope.
On a flowery veranda they sun themselves
azure and terra cotta. They are what we sail to
only to swerve: our beacon, goal, and warning.

The jeweled sight spells danger. I apply
for maps, for charts, for any boundary
to show where one thing ends, the next begins,
where both give way to water. Now two ships,

we and another, x on the noon-blazed ocean.
A dolphin scrambles from a dimpled pool
to chase a woman onto our empty deck.
She sloshes up full stairwells. Rats run after.

\*   \*   \*

Partition down. Stale whiffs of cellar clay
puff up cold clouds of dust.
A face grins out of the wall.
Tight little gusts of fury lie behind
nocturnal creaks and knockings.
Sisters beneath the fur, the cats and I
explore antinomies through the silent hours.
Old/young, spayed/fecund, big/small,
turbulent/tranquil—this one above all.
Like shoppers, one by one we take them up,
fingering private pleasures, kinds of grief.
One rages and one sleeps. I try on both.
I probe this glove of nerves from pole to pole.
If water is the substance of the soul,
dual dangers beckon, Scylla and Charybdis—
both deadly and no way to steer between them.
Always so far the whirlpool's first to choose.
And yet . . . the surface calm, tall clouds
sail over milky glass.
Ripples flicker and fade.
Shadows take root in every pond and puddle.
Stay still a little. See the half-lives
quietly swimming in the smallest fire-pond.

\*   \*   \*

As when we stood on a burning deck
and my companion—no, no *thing* was burning.

Flames flickered from the ocean. Someone said
it wasn't likely I would set on fire

the watery world we barely kept afloat in.
*No* fire was the trouble. We were soaking

and in one boat. Abruptly wet to the chin,
flesh of whose flesh, I tried to meet the gaze,

somber and piercing, and I dropped my eyes.
To what was said of my idea for signals

I had no answer, but looked out to sea.
Absence of islands there reminded me

of this story a marooned
musician told me once:

*   *   *

I was marooned, deserted in a frail
canoe with rival scores.
Only this bone-thin boat
shielded me from the terrible blue water.

Something was on the tip of my tongue.
Clock like, I struck my forehead in alarm.
Who purloined what? The notes that caulked
the cracks, kept out the water—

harmonies that repelled
the sharks and squid and kept my frame intact—
had I after all no right to them?
Wasn't the music mine?

The worst had happened. I woke up deserted,
far from the burning water,
floating on a raft of stolen songs.
No banner from a palm tree said *Come home*.

# Reconnaissance

What color was the ocean?

    A place, no color. There we made our vows.

What color was the ocean?

    Greyhound and driftwood melting into clouds.
    Sand the surf stroked and took its hand away.

What color was the ocean?

    Slate, neutral, battleship—some kind of grey
    except that it became a sheet of light
    when sun leaked down. Also it snored all night.

What color was the ocean?

    I never really knew. I had to turn
    around, repace the boardwalk to make sure.
    No colors filtered through the milky glare,
    not even heat, just (hours later) burn.

What color was the ocean?

    That afternoon
    (sky cradling a dim sun, a skinny moon)
    I went to look again and get it right.
    A mist was rising. Where the sand got wet
    I turned and looked behind me. There you were—
    a hundred yards away? but skeins of air
    tangled around you, smothering as smoke.
    Later you said you'd waved and called my name;
    I couldn't see a gesture, much less read a look.
    Out of the haze a Frisbee seemed to rise
    spontaneously, veering in slow motion.

I couldn't stay to see if it was caught.
My business was to gaze and learn by heart
once and for all the color of the ocean.
But there's no word for what I brought away
under my lids: not green, not brown, not grey,
not winedark glancing into points of light,
not glints of gunmetal dull or sharp as sky streamed
    dark or bright.

The sand was wet. We paced out silent vows,
then turned our backs on water and went into the
    house.

# Fog

*To See through Fog*

Horizon blotted out by fog, the world
blurs to a lowest common lump of cold
clay underneath one's feet, a chilly nub
hooed and hallooed at by incessant foghorns.
They say it will burn off.
To burn this broth of rust and milk and salt
is to ignite a cloud, set fire to water.

Seeing the least thing clearly thus becomes
a hopeless goal. Yet since there are no shadows
dancing in meadows, let me try to part
the blistery mist curtains, frame one face.
Omens of death have fluttered all week long
like starved mosquitoes through the soupy air.
Let me pierce fog-sheets down to the first scar.

*Low Tide*

A furtive slurp reveals the seamy side.
Spread seaweed dries to ochre of old brass,
gleaming yet dull, and salty shards of glass
appear like teeth. As if ten feet of water
could break the fog spell, fix the rare enamel
of precious days, I want it to be over,
the soggy process, thick nutritious smell,
the too slow rhythm of this heavy lapping.

Naked and bald, the beach is begging: *Add
water and serve if you want brightness now.*

All week high tide's at night. A full moon pulls
a rope of pearls through blackness. In our skulls
a summer's substance wavers under water.
We're full of food and sleep. We brim with dreams.

## No Change of Weather

Leprous-barked bushes lean and gleam with wet.
Matches won't light and salt won't pour. Keys stick:
piano, typewriter, even door.
Death in the house: the old tick tweezers straddle
idle in their glass jar. The orange cat
survives, arthritic: stroke him and he'll drool.
The page I write on now is of a piece
with the day's air, listless, floppy, cool.

In one wet week the summer leaches out
its shimmerings, its distance.
Cannot each sunny day or ten hours' sleep
be stowed away in deepest secrecy,
restored at need by "open sesame"?
I want a way to store the beauty up.


## To Sell the House?

Fryeburg, Naples, Paris, Elsinore:
tall gaunt white houses, their *For Sale* signs braving
the twilight. One imagines empty attics
whose wooden floors were star-marked once in dust
by the cold delicate feet of mice at midnight.
Nothing is even swept until a prospective buyer
suddenly looms from who knows where
to look the old place over.

His passage leaves a clammy signature
on each glass statuette. In every bedroom
he fogs the mirrors. And we still don't know
what he decided (this was years ago).
We're waiting, but his name is never mentioned.
Exiled ourselves, there are some things we exile.

*Late in the Day*

Atlantis sank, and Nineveh and Tyre
collapsed in earthquakes, whirlwinds, rains of ash.
The Dead Sea Scrolls were bundled out of sight.
The fierce brown sandstorm of that heavenly wrath
turned tribes to pretzels. Gritty civilization,
kneaded through aeons to a yeasty mess,
you've soaked to mildness in our steely water.
Windshieldlike, the palimpsest fogs over.

A cocoa-colored poodle
sprawls in our path like a prayer rug.
"Time to reread *Cities of the Plain*,"
you say as we go by through fog and rain.

Last night I dreamed of fire. Yes, again.
The wicked flourished and went sucking down.


*Brief Returns to the Nest*

For years of winters, weeks of precious summers,
the chaste old beds are empty.
Sudden, imperious, the children descend.

"If we can't sleep together we take the next boat out."

"What happens after I have gone to bed
is not my business, but she has the guest room,
young man. You sleep upstairs."

Still they come back, refuel, absorb their fill
of sea, sun, moon, of foghorn, mew of gull.
A watchful love awaits them and supports
their heavy bodies as the wind a gull.

Lazily soaring, they come down to earth
gently in time for yet another meal,
to face a shrunken reckoning later, later.


*Mother and Son*


A star through fog. Some sky. The table cleared,
I slip outside to glimpse the flaming fragments
and see them through the window, candle-lit,
profiled: a man and woman locked in combat.

Years of interrupting one another
have worn them down to bone, a gradual amputation.

Nothing sad can touch him: my old age,
the rising cost of houses, the dog dead,
the neighbor's daughter dying, loss on loss.

Doesn't she see it's Margaret she mourns for?
To give this mausoleum light and air,
first I'd get rid of the statuette collection.

A golden age is over. As the stronger will
flicks a chill wing on her face, I go back in.


*Visit of Dorothea Brooke, Seferis, Orwell, Chekhov, Thurber*


The ferryboat approaches, packed with souls.
Palely they squint throught mist.
Voices rise and gibber over the leaden water.

Like the red bunting on her Roman tour,
woolly and red and spreading everywhere,
the soaking green ubiquity of trees
seems to the solemn woman an ocular disease.

Smyrna. My father's house. I cannot bear
to see this place again: I knew it all.

The only dreadful changes are in me,
but everything is suddenly so small.

When can we leave the sticks and go to Moscow?

This weather is so strange. I hate this weather.
Why is it so hard to stay together?

*Weather Breaks*

And when the fog has lifted
how bland and pale the islands after all
appear as one by one they rise in daylight.
Low stony hills curtseying into the bay—
Burnt, Mouse, the Cuckolds, Squirrel, Negro, Ram—
only the names survive a change of weather.

The questing souls return in disappointment
to a mainland today so plain and clear
no myths can be rewoven out of cloud.

Back in the house unclaimed as yet by the anonymous
    buyer,
we're left alone. A little pool of silence
reflects us looking long at one another.
There is no need to name it, the gale that rocks the boat,
that rising gust choked down in every throat.

# III

*Locked in an Aorist Amber*

# Pantoum on Pumpkin Hill

The goldenrod sheds pollen in the butter.
The lawnmower, just before it stops, goes sputter.
The valleys echo roars from the wood cutter.
I write a word down; mouth it; finally utter.

The lawnmower, just before it stops, goes sputter.
My mother sinks to sleep with gentle snores.
I write a word down; mouth it; finally utter.
Quiet is sifting in from out of doors.

My mother sinks to sleep with gentle snores.
The typewriter cricket clicks its code.
Quiet is sifting in from out of doors.
The white cat pounces at a tardy toad.

The typewriter cricket clicks its code.
Upstairs you pace, you halt, you mark out time.
The white cat pounces at a tardy toad.
I chew a fingernail and find a rhyme.

Upstairs you pace, you halt, you mark out time.
Stand on the balcony, survivors; stare
(I chew a fingernail and find a rhyme)
At something time has no more terrors for.

Stand on the balcony, survivors; stare.
Never before have I dug quite so deep
At something time has no more terrors for
Beyond the honeyed film of summer sleep.

Never before have I dug quite so deep.
The world is fragile, old, and very small
Beyond the honeyed film of summer sleep
I follow syllable by syllable.

The world is fragile, old, and very small.
We've shrunk to dolls, our rhetoric's a mutter
I follow syllable by syllable:
The goldenrod sheds pollen in the butter.

# Siesta in the Summer House

Long lines breathe and swell in a rhythm I spin
almost to vanishing and pick up again. Successive risings
ripple and dimple, shrug, subside, rekindle. . . .
Muggy and mythy, afternoon extends its tingling filaments
all down a body, down to the toes that make themselves
    freshly felt.
Mushroom-quick flora of dampness, yeasty press of
    making.
Delicious to lie down as in a cave beside my mate
after the daily trotting off in opposite directions.
Nightly we nuzzle and roll and curl in familiar hollows,
but this hour after lunch is richer than sleep, it stretches
    like taffy,
the sun stops, voices blur and circle, everything goes slow.
Whose is that breathing next to me? You. You.


Downstairs the unborn kittens are being lugged around
in their little sacs of water by fluffy Pandora, heavy but
    skittish
on thundery afternoons like this one. Sparks and gusts of
    electricity
flicker through humid rooms although no lights are on.
Tiny shocks, pinprick sparks are wound in the skein of
    drowsing
that tangles us all but Pandora. Belly ballooned, pink
    nipples
arrowhead-sharp, she heaves herself in and out of bureau
    drawers,
climbs into the laundry hamper and hoists herself out
    again,
sways upstairs and then down, tugged all over the house
    by subterranean
changes all ready to arch and gleam from their cloudy
    tank of stillness,

leap and explode into visibility, flash like fish.
But it happens deep in the night.
Next morning the air is a little
clearer—water, say, poured into a bowl of honey—
and my mother is climbing the stairs and carefully peering
around the half-open bedroom door and saying
with an almost raffish triumph tamped down in her
    manner,
"There's been an addition." And we rush down to see
four kittens crawling nosing rooting snuggling squirming
    squeaking
starting their thirty-six lives in an ecstasy of siestas.

# Women Are Best for Feeding Cattle

being tender-hearted, says the manual
on animal husbandry.
Husbandry?
Never, sisterhood of the udder,
motherhood, udderhood, phalanx of hot flanks.
In the warm body, barn I never leave,
I feel your breathing: it could be my own,
your hunger's mine. I kiss your velvet muzzle,
I bathe in your warm urine, oh my sister.

Why should I speak at all?
A moo says everything.
Ours is the world of shit and milk.
Padding, milk pudding upholstering our chests
unites us, tit sisters,
slippery pink young
tonguing our outlets,
own warm faucets.

Only lactating mothers need apply.
If you sliced our chests,
milk and blood would mingle oh so gently
into the pink of roses, noses, cherries,
pink of little girls' dresses.

# Mothers

## I*

My love, you were a child; my child, you are a man now.
Go on, my darling, do not let the tempest overtake you.

Mother, look; night has fallen. How can I go? It's
   raining.
Mother, sorrow keeps me here, a kind of terror clamps
   me.

My child, they're all departing now—and will you be the
   last one?
Go on; be foremost always, always beautiful.

Mother, winter's trickling in and night is coming on.
Shame ties me down, distress pursues me.

My child, look forward; do not let the past embitter you.
Life like a horse is champing at the door.

Mother, the wind has blown the plane tree down across
   the road.
Memory devours me, the past gnaws me.

My child, they're all departing now—and will you be the
   last one?
Go on; be foremost always, always beautiful.

Mother, look, night has fallen. How can I go? It's
   raining.
Mother, sorrow keeps me here, a kind of terror clamps
   me.

*Part I is a translation from the Greek of Kostas Karyotakis (d. 1928).

## II

Dimly we peer from under heaped
counterpanes, old indulgences.

Every morning it happens again.
Stale eddies are gingerly stirred

by white wings' snick and flutter,
swoop, sweep through thick clutter,

succor of years and years
they fed and tended us.

Accumulated nurture
lets no one break the habit.

In all their tender comings and goings
they never once expect to be told to stop,

to pause in mid-trajectory,
see us glance brightly up.

# Filial

You've left the garden, gone away to pay
the debt we owe all fathers and all mothers
whose sands are running out,
all those who near the end of the voyage leaned
over the rail to gaze at the sun-flushed water
and see what flickered. Ah, she bent too low!
Artemis' gentle arrows pushed her over.
She lurches back toward shore. And will you meet those
    eyes
and tell her summer's ripe outside her window?

One thing is left her. Though the busy seed
of appetite's gone finite in her head,
words do remain, a lifetime's stock of language
stored against need, translucent jar on jar
stacked in a deep dark cellar. But a weary syntax
chips down to baby talk not words but hours
slower and slower: syl by a by ble
silly bull sibyl able sibling label
to hapaxes we stumble at. The flow
slowed to a trickle, you stop dead. Come home.

# Praise for a Patch of Quiet

Two of the strongest silences to lean on:
a white cat lying on a wooden floor
waking to stretch and stretching back to sleep
(cream walls, grey-painted floorboards, plain white
    curtains,
black metronome)
and out of doors where all the world's a timepiece
this slope of ripening or ripened apples.
Their floating tart perfumes do not insist
to one whose only hunger is for quiet
this afternoon; they just enrich the air,
invisibly adorn one's breathing space.

Spaces between first words, then conversations:
the tempo slows. Rust holes at first
glinted like isolate stars in the tin barn roof
years have dappled since
to slow transparency.
I'd thought to be alone would be . . . would be . . .
bees buzzed a busy swarm, each mote a menace.
Would be to lose a writing hand, a face,
a sounding board, a listening ear, a voice—
all lopped imaginings. Would be and was
and is this afternoon to lose the need
for ticktock voicing. Silence
thickens: mercury
gleams afresh in the cherished tarnished mirror
I tilt, across whose valuable sheen
as over clean white paper
half a dozen summer
pencils lightly scribble:
insect buzz, chainsaw, birdcall, hoot of train,
pattern simple at once and multiple
as are the endless changes of attention
due to a single hour of cloudboats sailing
across and across a shifting summer sky.

Sun sidles under
a cloud; the silence darkens.
No longer floating, sleepy sounds tune up
for a composite thunderclap and downpour
offstage as yet. A crow's *shrike shrike*
rips clear through a shimmering maple veil.
Awakening, the cat
knows she must compose a sleek new self
from wisps and curls of sleep.
She starts to lick herself in preparation.

# Dry Season

~~~~~~~~~~~~~~~~~~~~~~~~~~~~~~~~~~~~~~~~~~~~~~~~~

Flip back and forth, the gritty hours—this deeply rooted
    book
whose pages gauge the seasons of the house
swaying on their long stems through a dry time.
No flow but what we furnished, rank and warm
whether in summer's lap or autumn's dustbowl
or on the shining stones of early winter
or weathered barn boards soft as blotting paper.
We peed at every hour in every weather
under the sky, at dawn behind the lilacs
or noon under the apple tree or moonlight
right in the road. Mornings we took our trowels
and headed up separate paths to the pine woods
where fragrant needles were an easily acquired
matrix. One day the cat
followed you up and caught and lost again
a mole burrowing under the needles:
you crapped and watched.
From time to time we lay down flat to peer into the well.
A single stub of pencil
plummeted from some pocket
insolently winked from a dry bottom.
Well, shut the lid. We did, and for a time
forgot the dream of flowing.
All things flow in their own way, according
to their own time, as time, or even in time,
if you can find a place to stand apart and so perceive it.

That was the year of my persistent hemorrhoid.
Soaking was prescribed. I used to sit
for twenty minutes twice a day behind
the house in a plastic tub of heated water
hauled from the spring, reading or playing Scrabble
with you. The box ran red onto the dampened pieces:
a purple *n* or *u* brings back that time.
Up down, up down—the old motifs. The cat
discovered a rural preference for prefab
concavities—say a hoofprint—
daintily into which to defecate
on morning strolls. The leafless branches made
apples glint like little chips of topaz
hills showed clear through—yet distances drew in.
The cows grew fuzzier and stood more closely packed,
steaming through their nostrils. Rifle shots
seemed louder. One hour's distance from the hearth
filled each of us with news to tell the other.
Smell of woodsmoke. Certain sunny mornings
made the room brim with radiance, like a grail.

# Five September Hours

*Feeding the Birds*

Lured by unnatural feeding,
by promises of plenty lavishly
sprinkled and arced and scattered on cold weather,
even the tufted titmouse
has recently been known
to loiter in the north here into winter.
To feed or not to feed? The weather lady
is careful, subtle, noncommittal, anxious:
"I'm sure more studies must be needed, but
if you can't keep on feeding through the winter,
it really may be better not to start.
It's something for us all to think about."

*Reflection*

Intent at my desk after breakfast,
head down or gazing out at infinities,
I manage to ignore the sudden brilliance of the moment
the fog burns off and all the jewels of morning
are finally free to flash and burst and twinkle.
But it won't do. The very windowpane
I look through blankly, focusing on nothing,
holds up a still life from over my shoulder.
Honey pot, mug, George's tobacco jar—
chess pieces poised on the red and white
checks of the tablecloth? Good burghers
burnished with sun as they keep house in space?
Even as ghosts, all radiate well-being.
Strange, though, the inky shadows
poured from each object as it's illumined.
Unbargained for, they catch my eye and hold me
after I look away. The gems of morning

still coruscate. Their brightness gives me back
the sun-soaked still life mirrored by the window
sliced to gay ribbons by the shadows' black.


*Going for Water*

Our well is dry; we use the spring for water.
Down from a slope beside the railroad trestle
the water trickles into a rusty barrel.
"You drink that water?" asks a passing driver
slowing a moment. "You know, the railroad sprays,"
and makes to go. "Sprays for what?" "Oh, everything.
Weeds." He accelerates. "Well, anyway,
I guess it is something to think about."
No answer but a red squirrel's sudden manic chatter
above the slow brown flow of leaf-flecked water.


*Picking Flowers*

A late bee in the faded goldenrod
or washed-out asters clutches
the August ghosts I'm wandering in search of
(blue of old denim, faintest shred of fragrance)
and when I take a step and snap the stalk
and carry off September's tattered colors
downhill and home, the bee,
confused or dogged, hovering around beside behind me,
follows the armload that's left of summer
a desperate distance—through the door, into the room,
up to the lip of the cracked and mended pitcher
we always use for Queen Anne's Lace, Joe-Pye-Weed,
    Black-Eyed Susan,
on whose side a spray of goldenrod
waves deathlessly its perfect porcelain bloom.

*Moonlight*

Hard frost tonight, first night of fall, first full
moon riding across the Northeast Kingdom,
but after a golden day of Indian summer
the roof and walls have hardly yet begun to cool.
Under the blankets we sweat in our long johns.
Get up, says the small chill
medallion of moon. Come to the window.
Come downstairs. See me. Greet me.
In all my royal progress through the county,
my pauses, poises, arcs, and visitations,
I have seen fit to shine
onto your checkered tablecloth. Come down.

True: she's transformed its field of red and white
to sharp unblinking squares of murk and bright,
clear enough, one would think, to read by, or to write.
I take a book. But no.
My hand's steep slant of shadow
crosses a glimmering page awash with pearl.
Letters and words remain illegible
as conversation heard from the next room
(voices may rise in anger or grumble low in gloom,
but not a single phrase comes clearly through the wall).

I eat a shadowy apple: not red, just steely sheen.
Abstracting all the implements of night
into a polar pull of black and white,
a magic bandage swathes the room till dawn.
Goggled in dimness, I begin to yawn.
Drowsily a thin mist veils the moon.
Upstairs again. But lady, until day
let me give my dreams into your keeping
whose perfect pallor bleeds the black from sleep.

# Moving Still

Already I'm October's passenger.
Flat field, tangle of drying
vetch at the hedges, oaks and maples
dipped bough by bough in melted bronze,

green spread of lawn behind me,
wet feather drooping willow fingers
touched by late sun can break a heart.
I wrap myself therefore

apple-tight in skin,
my cover and container, sometimes thin
to vanishing, but there, but tough, but mine,
no random dropcloth hastily flung on.

Before this dark blue season there was fragrant
September. Now the cool
curve of the tenth month's fruitbowl
braces me. From its shadow

I crane at racing clouds,
breathe rare air, radiant. It is possible
to see a silo tall in deepening light,
to drop the reins, be carried on and on.

# Four Dreams about the Same Fortress

*Fall*

Bare boughs of a fall forest. Close-up: black
peelings of primer dangle from a wall.
Besieged within, we women hold them back.

Who? The invaders on their ladders. Tall
men claw at the windows of the tower
and wave their arms and stagger back and fall.

We should be free by twilight. Shadows lower
in the unlighted room and turn us brown,
hands, faces. We are glad, but lack the power

to send a message to the nearest town
that we're imprisoned in our citadel,
victorious but with no way to get down.

*Winter*

Low brick-dark sky rimmed by adobe dawn.
Pursuit and exile, flight and fear and loss.
Lines as of trolleys crisscrossing the plaza
and distant lightning and a torsoed mob
hammering at the windows. Oh, we crossed
the cocoa highway, pounded in our turn
at a dark door and waited while the drapes
stirred softly. They were watching us, of course.
Violet from a valley
the winter sun rose and a door was opened.
Through maroon curtains
we made our way to temporary shelter.

*Spring*

How little the place has changed,
perhaps a trifle tidier.
Courage! No one has broken in this time.
Come summer, we'll move into it again.
But after all a portent on the lawn.
My old toy chest, its splintery barn-red boards
covered with pink-sprigged wallpaper—
tender protection, yes,
and another of the endless disguises—
it is half empty. Ice skates,
bits of paper wadded tight in corners
look stranded. They have taken
the marionettes, the mothball-smelling blankets.
My fears had been for the locked attic room.
But this toy chest, the way it gapes at light—
an hourglass half run out.

*Summer*

| | | |
|---|---|---|
| old territorial | rock and water | cave combat |
| two women | dark and fair | hurl insults |
| bloodwarm water | oyster grain | balances a rowboat |
| patron of angers | slammed door | scale of dangers |
| draw a line | cat on piano | stamps black notes |
| here ends | flash of recognition | here begins |
| crone steals sheets | sky/crack/light | empty bed |

# Speaking in Tongues

It is one and two and three
and close to four. No use
trying to sleep. I pad
down the hall. I heat
milk in a little brown enameled pan
*Made in Poland.* Poland, sealed-off place.
Something is rotten in the state of Poland.
I stir in Nestlé's Quik, my feet
frigid on the black, white,
and grey linoleum floor,
which is blistered like skin from the time
some butter caught on fire
in this same saucepan. Memories—
pain, otherness, delight—
seep into me tonight
up from my two cold feet
as water through a pore.
I may not be able to sleep
but there are circumstances I can hold
against me through my nightgown in the cold.
My nightgown. I look down:
I thought it was sprigged with pink
but even for four A.M.
it looks pretty pale and wan.
Oh. It's inside out.
I must have put it on
blindly in the dark.
I had been reading the old tongue again,
was back in the undertow, moving fast and frightened,
was trellised like a vine, branched and directed.
What was this edifice

whose humblest terrace I was trained to cover?
My family? my language? or not mine?
Through thick winter black
nostalgia winked a knowing wink,
even when I had sprung from bed,
flung on my nightgown, hurried to the dead
kitchen, and was standing by the sink.
Figures sped by me, faceless.
They skimmed—or something skimmed—years off my
    life,
so much scum from the top of a cooling cup!
Now in the pan the cocoa raises up
its head like a cobra, hisses,
swells with self-importance.

# Marriage Rhapsody

to George

No one could paint how green July is here.
Lollipops, shamrocks, trading stamps
are not too bright but wrong
as wax apricots; lack lambency.
Take the green ground where they stood in a sunlit circle,
one in white gauze not knowing where to aim
the heart's rapt, dumb attention.

Dear place, each glacial lump so memorized—
it happened, and the calendar continued
the cleaving, breathing, sleeping, letting go.
One difficulty always was the mere
assimilation of so pure an air.
Surely it ought to be enough
to have learned the geometric
progression of pine trees growing,
to have glimpsed the great white rabbit flopping
through fading woods at dusk.
Buried bones in the hill.
Bees in the thyme.
The bolt of livid lightning
making us scatter off the tennis court.
Wasn't it enough
to have gathered bridal flowers in the cow field
and have come home and seen the big and little cats
curled yin-yang on the porch in a pool of sun?

As if a creature long in hibernation
should shake itself awake,
a heavenly flaw appeared at noon, a sudden
gulf of candor opening like clouds
to close again. The freshly cut
grass glistened green as glass.

A mother swallow looped and swerved to the chicks
hungrily chuckling and clucking in the birdhouse,
a heraldic penguin waddled out of sight
behind the lilac where the kingbird cheeped
his being, being, being
somehow in a single note.

Before dawn in a dim quartet of hours
you are the cello, I'm a violin,
and when I try to spoon my knees behind you,
arm to your hip, you wriggle and complain
I'm imitating you—the way you lie,
sleep, move, your very breathing.
*A taste of the lash*, you mutter under your breath
unless I'm imagining things.
Anyway I roll over and wonder.
Isn't intertwining
what canons are all about?
Even the ten weeks' kitten
curls herself precisely
behind the huffy Siamese dowager
rigid with emulation.
These subtle sympathies and leaping currents,
energies of art: if you whack a tough
steak with a croquet mallet to make it tender,
do I then rush upstairs and scribble down a sonnet?
Better to smash the mirror of a symmetry like that
than suck the precious juice from every gesture.
Meanwhile the incubus is struggling out of
the same old shrunken garment.
A ghost that sometimes wears a name and face
speaks the old language sadly, and I tell it
*I have nothing against you,*
*but will you please get out of here for good?*

*This is my house.* And someone
empties a glass of ouzo over its head,
icy tinkle that ought to turn to bird song.
It's getting light.

But it turns out to be an auspicious sneeze
that wakes the bridal couple on the morning.
And soon the buttercup-bright array assembles over the
    lawn . . .
Take away the album.
Having is holding. For that space of time
the bugs stopped humming and the sun stood still.
Dressed in white, forgetting to remember,
she blinked in the sun. Later baby's breath
withered in the bouquet, but words remain,
locked in an aorist amber.
Ceremony is stoppage, petrification
of layers that have been accumulating with all their fossils;
and it is a dipper scooped into a dimpling flow,
ripple and wink. The reaching hands emerge
cool, wet, and empty.

Nothing is ever enough.
Heavy water cautiously balanced in a pitcher
spills on the flesh and sears it down to bone.
Let the right blood have been broken in the test tube,
the wrong blood solemnly recorded in a book of law,
my flesh, my brand-new bloodmate. If that's what makes a
    wedding,
they framed us into fact. No, we ourselves
stood ringed with wishes. If it wasn't written
for us, let me have said
that as at the end of a fairy tale
the marriage was accomplished.
But this is not the end.

## About the Author

Rachel Hadas was graduated from Radcliffe College with a
B.A.; from Johns Hopkins with an M.A., and from Princeton
University with a Ph.D. in comparative literature. After
Radcliffe, she helped run an olive oil press in Greece and, in
1974, was indicted and tried for, and acquitted of arson in
connection with a mysterious fire at the press. Her poems have
appeared in a chapbook, *Starting from Troy* (1975), and in *The
Atlantic, The New Yorker, Harper's, Poetry,* and other magazines.
She teaches English at Rutgers University in Newark, New
Jersey, and lives in Manhattan and St. Johnsbury, Vermont.

## About the Book

The text and display type are Caslon Old Face #2. Composi-
tion and typesetting were done by G&S Typesetters of
Austin, Texas. The book was printed on 60 lb. Warren's
Olde Style paper and bound in Holliston Roxite by Kingsport
Press, Kingsport, Tennessee.
Design and production were by Joyce Kachergis Book Design
& Production, Bynum, North Carolina.